Understanding the Science of

VCR

and How They Works

A Journey Through the Mechanics and Legacy of VHS in the Digital Age

Victor M Tom.

Table of contents

Introduction

In a world constantly moving forward with new advancements in digital streaming, artificial intelligence, and high-definition devices, there's something very compelling about looking back at the technology that sets the groundwork for today's media. Among these analog relics, the VCR stands out as a home entertainment icon, bringing movie enchantment from the big screen to living rooms worldwide. The buzz of its mechanical gears, the click of a tape loading, and the whirring sounds when it fast-forwards or rewinds all add to its allure. These familiar sounds and movements generate nostalgia in those who grew up with the gadget, as well as curiosity in younger generations who may have only seen a VCR in an old movie or the back of a junk store. This book brings readers into the world of the VCR, not simply as a piece of equipment, but as a symbol of a bygone era.

Controlling what to watch—and when to view it—was an exciting novelty.

This exploration is more than just reminiscence; it's an in-depth look at how the VCR operated. From the delicate process of threading tape around the drum to the meticulous science of recording and playback, the VCR was a technological marvel of its time. This book seeks to decipher the inner workings of this once-revolutionary technology, demonstrating how each component contributed to the experience of watching movies and shows on demand. By delving into these intricacies, the book uncovers the genius underlying analog gadgets, their mechanical perfection, and the rich, hands-on connection they provide—unlike today's passive experience with digital media. Understanding the VCR involves not only revisiting a piece of entertainment history but also appreciating a time when technology gave the viewer a sense of agency, a connection to the moving parts and processes that enabled each viewing experience.

This book is intended for those who enjoy peeling back the layers of technology to understand how it works. It's for readers who enjoy the allure of vintage gadgets and the combination of science, physics, and design. Whether you're a tech enthusiast looking to learn about analog devices, a nostalgia seeker recalling the glory days of VHS tapes, or simply someone fascinated by the evolution of entertainment, this book provides a window into the world of VCRs with clarity, simplicity, and the same sense of discovery that these machines inspired in their prime. Through this journey, we'll not only look at how the VCR worked but also at its legacy and long-term impact, paying tribute to a gadget that changed how we experienced visual narrative, one reel of magnetic tape at a time.

Chapter 1: An Overview of VCRs and VHS

In the early days of cinema, seeing a film was an experience reserved for theaters, where the wonder of moving pictures was displayed on a large screen. For decades, this was the only means for audiences to experience visual narrative. To see a movie, people had to leave their houses, often traveling to crowded movie theaters with rows of seats, big curtains, and large screens that generated an atmosphere of excitement and anticipation. It was a community event, and the joy of viewing a movie with other people became a popular kind of entertainment. However, this structure meant that viewing options were limited to what theaters offered, and consumers could only see a film when it was playing in theaters.

As technology advanced, the possibility of bringing this experience into the home became more apparent. In the 1950s, the arrival of black-and-white television sets revolutionized everything.

Allowing families to view news, shows, and live events without leaving their living rooms. Suddenly, the concept of personal, on-demand viewing became increasingly viable. Television provided a more intimate experience, allowing individuals to see programming at home, albeit limited to what was broadcast at the time. As television became a household staple, it introduced entertainment, sports, and news into living rooms, ushering in the era of home viewing. Color televisions emerged in the 1960s, improving the viewing experience and making it more visually appealing.

Despite these advancements, viewers were still limited by broadcast times. They couldn't pause, rewind, or rewatch programs, so they had to watch them live. The desire to record, preserve, and playback video content sparked a significant advancement in home entertainment technology. Companies began to experiment with magnetic tape, a material capable of storing both audio and visual data, allowing broadcasts to be recorded and replayed. The

The original home video recorders were huge, expensive, and impracticable for general household usage, frequently designated for professional use in television studios. However, this was only the beginning.

By the 1970s, developers tried to make video technology more accessible to the general public. Efforts resulted in the development of equipment capable of playing pre-recorded programming or even recording live broadcasts to tapes. These developments paved the way for the Video Cassette Recorder (VCR). For the first time, people could record and watch television shows, movies, and personal recordings on their own time. This change from theater-exclusive experiences to home-based video technology ushered in a new era of entertainment, offering people more control over what and when they viewed it.

Television revolutionized home entertainment by allowing individuals to watch moving images in their own homes.

Rooms. Early television sets in the 1930s and 1940s showed black-and-white broadcasts, which, despite their lack of color, provided a sense of wonder and novelty. Watching live news, sports, and other events develop at home was exciting, and television quickly became a symbol of modern life, bringing the world into people's homes. However, these early broadcasts lacked the vitality and depth that moviegoers saw in theaters. Despite the limited color palette, black-and-white television quickly gained popularity, and TVs became more inexpensive and prevalent in families all over the world.

The introduction of color television in the 1950s represented a significant step forward, providing a new level of excitement to the viewing experience. With the introduction of color, television programs became more lifelike, engaging viewers in ways that black-and-white graphics could not. Shows, movies, and ads became more visually appealing, making home entertainment more engaging and captivating.

Color televisions were initially more expensive, but as technology advanced, they became more affordable to households. This color transition not only altered how people perceived television but also spurred a continuing demand for advances in home entertainment.

By the 1960s, television had cemented its place as a home staple, and there was a growing desire for greater control over content. While color added dimension, viewers were still confined by broadcasters' schedules, unable to pick what or when to watch. People could only watch shows when they aired, and there was no ability to replay favorites or save memorable broadcasts. This limitation fueled a demand for technologies that gave viewers control, resulting in a wave of innovation centered on capturing and replaying content.

As television evolved in the late 1970s, the Video Cassette Recorder (VCR) arose as a solution to the growing desire for flexibility. The

VCRs used existing magnetic tape technology, which had been perfected over years of development, to allow viewers to record television shows and play pre-recorded movies at home. This leap was made possible in part by the standardization of the VHS (Video Home System) tape format, which became popular because of its capacity and low cost. VHS tapes enabled consumers to own movies and record live broadcasts, allowing them to create personal libraries and consume content on their terms.

The transition from black-and-white to color television paved the way for the VCR by broadening the scope of home entertainment and encouraging people to invest in more immersive and flexible viewing options. As color television became the standard, viewers were ready for the next level of interaction: the ability to manage, save, and replay their favorite material. This change in television produced the ideal climate for the VCR to flourish, ushering in a new era where viewers may

Enjoy entertainment on their terms, whenever they wish.

As the concept of recording and playing back videos at home gained traction in the 1970s, two key formats arose, both seeking to become the standard in home video technology: VHS (Video Home System) and Betamax. JVC developed VHS, which rapidly met a strong opponent in Betamax, a format produced by Sony. Both formats had similar characteristics, allowing users to record television shows and watch movies on cassette tapes, but they differed in numerous important ways. This fight between VHS and Betamax became one of the most prominent format wars in consumer electronics, with VHS eventually emerging victorious thanks to a combination of practical and market-driven considerations.

One of the primary reasons VHS outperformed Betamax was recording duration. While Betamax initially provided somewhat better image quality, VHS tapes could store more content, recording up to two hours.

On a single tape, eventually extending to four or even six hours. This capability was particularly appealing to customers who wanted to record complete movies, sporting events, or lengthy TV broadcasts without using numerous tapes. VHS had an advantage in terms of convenience because of its extended recording period, which allowed viewers to capture and playback programming with minimal interruption.

Cost was also a big factor. Betamax machines were often more expensive, reflecting Sony's emphasis on quality and endurance, but this limited their availability to the average household. JVC, on the other hand, positioned VHS as a low-cost alternative, making its players and tapes more accessible. VHS became widely available, with numerous manufacturers adopting the technology and developing compatible players. This widespread availability and affordability drew more consumers to VHS, resulting in a stronger market presence. Video rental companies, a developing trend at the time, increasingly preferred VHS cassettes due to lower

Costs and a wider number of VHS-compatible players in households bolstered VHS's dominance.

By the 1980s, VHS had virtually won the format battle, and VCRs had become home staples, ushering in the golden age of the VCR. Throughout the 1980s and 1990s, families all around the world used VCRs to view movies and record television programming. Almost every town saw the emergence of video rental stores, which stocked shelves with VHS cassettes of popular movies, family favorites, and TV shows. The ability to rent movies and watch them at home provided an affordable source of entertainment, expanding watching options beyond television broadcasts. "Be Kind, Rewind" stickers were commonplace, encouraging renters to rewind tapes before returning them—a tiny ritual that became an integral part of the VHS experience.

In addition to rentals, VCRs allowed viewers to record live broadcasts, sporting events, and special programming. For the first time, people could.

Time-shift their watching schedules, allowing individuals to record episodes that air at inconvenient times and watch them later. Families could establish personal libraries of recorded shows and movies to view anytime they wanted, without having to adhere to television schedules. The VCR transformed home entertainment, allowing viewers unprecedented flexibility over what and when they watched.

However, by the early 2000s, the popularity of VCRs and VHS tapes had begun to dwindle. The DVD introduced a new format with higher picture quality, clearer sound, and more convenient features like scene selection and menu navigation. DVDs used less space were easier to store, and removed the need for rewinding. As DVDs became more affordable and popular, they swiftly displaced VHS tapes on store shelves and in rental stores. The transition was quick, and households started trading their VCRs for DVDs.

Players were anxious to take advantage of the better quality and simplicity that DVDs offered.

VCRs received their fatal blow when digital streaming became popular in the late 2000s and beyond. As internet connections improved and streaming platforms such as Netflix, Hulu, and subsequently Disney+ and Amazon Prime Video gained popularity, individuals no longer required physical media to access a massive collection of content. Streaming provided the convenience of watching movies and shows instantly, without the need for tapes or disks, and allowed viewers to select from a greater selection of options than ever before. The demand for physical media continues to fall, making VHS and VCRs obsolete in the mainstream.

While some aficionados and collectors still treasure VHS tapes and VCRs, the age of analog home video came to a close with the introduction of digital streaming. What once revolutionized how we received media is now viewed as a nostalgic piece of technology, a memento of a time when

Rewinding, fast-forwarding, and carefully handling tapes were all part of the experience. The emergence and fall of the VCR underscores the quick rate of technological advancement and the ever-changing nature of how we interact with tales on screen.

Chapter 2: Understanding the VHS Tape

At first glance, a VHS tape appears simple—just a plastic casing with few spools and a strip of tape—but each component is critical for storing and playing back film and audio. A VHS tape consists of two primary reels, a lengthy strip of magnetic tape, and a protective plastic shell to keep everything together. The reels are located on either side of the tape, and each plays a unique role during playback and recording. When the tape is played, it advances from the supply reel, where most of the tape is wound initially, to the take-up reel. This controlled movement ensures the tape runs smoothly, allowing it to be read uninterrupted. The casing is more than simply a protective shell; it also features a spring-loaded door that protects the fragile magnetic tape from dust and debris, which could destroy it. This door only opens when the tape is inserted into a VCR, providing an additional layer of safety.

The magnetic tape that stores the movie, show, or

recorded content is the true heart of the VHS tape. A magnetic tape is a narrow, black strip coated with a magnetic substance, usually iron oxide. This magnetic surface stores video and audio data in a manner comparable to that of cassette tapes, which became popular for music. During recording, the VCR's magnetic heads leave patterns on the tape that correlate to sound and images. As the tape passes by these heads, it stores information in the form of magnetic signals structured in different patterns. These patterns are extremely exact, recording both visual and audio data on the tape in a form that can be deciphered during playback.

The tape is separated into sections, each dedicated to a certain type of information. The middle section of the tape contains visual data, while the top section contains audio data. This arrangement ensures that both video and sound are recorded on the same strip, allowing for synchronized playback.

The magnetic signals contained in these portions are read by the VCR's heads and converted back into images and sounds, which are subsequently presented on the screen. This layered arrangement is what distinguishes VHS tapes, as they contain both moving images and clear sound on a single strip of tape that can be rewound, fast-forwarded, and replayed numerous times.

The VHS tape's architecture features various built-in systems to keep it secure and undamaged when not in use, including the reel lock and protective door mechanism. The reel lock is a basic but important function that keeps the reels from spinning freely while the tape is not in the VCR. This locking mechanism keeps the magnetic tape securely wound around the reels, preventing inadvertent unspooling, tangling, or damage. When you insert a tape into a VCR, a little piece of metal inside the machine pushes through an aperture in the tape's case, releasing the reel lock. This permits the reels to rotate as expected.

Providing smooth playback, rewinding, and fast-forwarding.

The door mechanism provides additional protection for the delicate magnetic tape. The front of the VHS cassette has a spring-loaded door that stays closed while the tape is not in use, protecting the magnetic tape from dust, debris, and light exposure, which can impair the tape's quality over time. When the cassette is introduced into a VCR, the machine activates a mechanism that gently opens this door, allowing the VCR's internal components to access the magnetic tape. Once the door is unlocked and the reel lock is disengaged, the VCR's guide rollers extract the tape from the cassette and thread it through the machine's reading heads. This preparation procedure occurs every time a tape is loaded, preparing the VCR to read the stored data.

The capacity and length of the magnetic tape within each VHS cassette are critical in deciding how much video content it can hold. VHS cassettes

Typically, they hold approximately 246 meters (800 feet) of magnetic tape. If completely unwound, this length is enough to stretch nearly halfway up the Eiffel Tower, demonstrating how much tape is crammed into each cassette. This tape length is intended to allow different recording speeds and lengths. Standard play (SP) mode allows for around two hours of video on a single tape, although extended play (EP) and long play (LP) modes can hold up to four or six hours, respectively. These longer recording modes result in lower video quality since more information is crammed onto the same length of tape.

Each inch of magnetic tape has a carefully layered sequence of audio and video data encoded as magnetic signals. The amount of content that can be saved and played back is determined by the overall length of the tape and the recording mode used. VHS was a versatile and convenient way to record movies, shows, and

Personal recordings. The reel lock, door mechanism, and long tape length work together to provide a functional, dependable storage device that has remained popular for decades.

Chapter 3: Key components within the VCR.

Inside a VCR, a complex array of mechanics and parts work together to bring a videotape to life on screen. These components are meticulously placed to accommodate the tape when it plays, rewinds, or fast-forwards. The VCR is built around a number of motors, gears, and rollers that are all connected via a central circuit board that controls the machine's processes. The carriage loading assembly, the drum with magnetic heads, guiding rollers, tension arms, the capstan and pinch roller, and an audio head are all essential components that must work together to read the fragile magnetic tape and create crisp, synchronized playback. The arrangement is intended to interact fluidly with a VHS tape from the moment it is inserted until it is ejected, resulting in a seamless watching experience.

The process begins with the carriage loading assembly, which allows a VCR to

Accept and position a VHS cassette for playing. When a cassette is introduced, the loading assembly guides it into place, securely gripping the tape and positioning it for use by the machine's internal components. Inserting the tape causes the VCR's loading mechanism to engage, and when the cassette is pushed inward, the assembly gently lowers it into the device. This movement is precise; a set of motors and gears precisely moves the tape to ensure it is properly aligned for playback. The spring-loaded door on the cassette opens as the loading mechanism lowers the tape, allowing the VCR to access the magnetic tape inside.

As the tape is completely lowered, the carriage assembly engages the guide rollers. These little rollers travel down curved tracks, taking the magnetic tape from within the cassette and threading it around the drum. The guide rollers are particularly engineered to interact with the VHS tape's allocated holes, allowing the magnetic tape to be accurately positioned along the playback path. This setup.

Guarantees the tape is taut and perfectly aligned with the VCR's reading heads. As the guide rollers pull the tape around the drum, they prepare the VCR to read the information stored on the tape, paving the way for smooth, continuous playback.

The loading process, which is completely controlled by the VCR's mechanical and electronic components, is critical to the machine's operation. The combination of the carriage loading assembly and the exact movement of the guide rollers results in a synchronized, automatic setup that allows the VCR to seamlessly transition between loading, playback, and ejection. This first handling of the tape is only the beginning, as each component of the VCR is now prepared to play its part in providing a fully functional watching experience.

A VCR's guide rollers play an important role in managing the delicate movement of the magnetic tape, extracting it from the reels and precisely directing it through the machine's internal track.

When a VHS tape is loaded, the guide rollers engage and slip into predefined slots at the bottom of the cassette, ensuring a secure grasp on the tape. These rollers are designed to move over specifically curved tracks, pulling the tape from the cassette and threading it around important components within the VCR, preparing it for playback. The tape is carefully stretched across the rollers, with exactly the correct amount of tension to prevent slippage or wrinkling, both of which can degrade video and audio quality.

The guide rollers pull the tape into position, ensuring that it follows an exact course around the VCR's primary components, such as the drum, capstan, and numerous heads. This carefully planned movement sets the tape at the best angle for each component to retrieve the stored data. The quality of this tape path is critical since even minor misalignments might cause signal distortions or loss. After the guiding rollers have sent the tape through the machine,

The VCR is prepared to read and interpret magnetic impulses, which are then turned into images and sounds on the screen.

The drum, a huge cylindrical component positioned slightly tilted within the VCR, is important to the reading process. This tilt may appear unusual at first, but it is purposeful and designed to improve the efficiency of reading the magnetic tape. The drum contains magnetic heads, which are crucial in decoding the information recorded on the tape. As the tape rolls across the drum, these heads make contact with the magnetic surface and scan it for information. The drum rotates quickly, roughly 1,800 rotations per minute, while the magnetic tape moves slowly, generating a speed difference that allows the heads to accurately read a dense amount of information.

The helical scan reading technique is dependent on the drum's tilted angle. This approach includes reading the magnetic impulses diagonally across the tape, rather than straight.

Across the width. This diagonal reading pattern makes better use of the tape's available area, allowing for more effective storage and reading of video data. As the drum spins, the heads follow these diagonal lines, deciphering and turning the recorded magnetic impulses into visual data. This exact alignment allows the VCR to recover and display a crisp, uninterrupted image on the screen.

The VCR can process and send video and music with remarkable consistency because the guide rollers, drum, and magnetic heads are all working in sync. Each component helps to create a smooth, seamless playback experience by converting the tape's magnetic signals into a real-time display of moving images and sound for the viewer. This complicated ballet of components demonstrates the ingenuity that has made the VCR a decades-long staple of home entertainment.

In addition to the guide rollers and drum, several

other important components inside a VCR contribute to

The magnetic tape moves smoothly and precisely. Each component has a unique purpose in ensuring that the tape moves smoothly through the machine, delivering a constant playing experience without interruptions.

The capstan is a tiny metal spindle that, along with the pinch roller, controls the speed of the tape as it passes across the heads. The capstan, located right after the drum, spins at a steady, regulated rate, ensuring that the tape advances through the machine at the proper speed for playback. Without this regular movement, the film and audio would become distorted because the tape would run too fast or too slowly.

The pinch roller, a rubber wheel placed right across from the capstan, keeps the tape tightly against it. This grip is vital for keeping the tape from sliding or diverting from its path. The pinch roller's soft surface allows it to exert just enough pressure to keep the tape moving smoothly while not hurting the fragile magnetic strip.

The capstan and pinch roller work together to provide a regulated, constant pull on the tape, ensuring clear and synchronized playback.

Tension arms, situated on either side of the tape route, provide an additional level of control. These arms use minimal pressure to hold the tape taut as it rolls around the drum and other components. The arms maintain steady strain, preventing the tape from drooping or becoming slack, which could cause it to shift out of alignment or wrinkle. Proper tension is essential for smooth playback and helps to maintain the tape's integrity over multiple uses.

Each of these components—the capstan, pinch roller, and tension arms—is critical to ensuring that the tape runs smoothly through the VCR without interruption or distortion. They work together to provide a steady environment in which the magnetic signals on the tape can be reliably read, allowing the VCR to provide a high-quality viewing experience.

Chapter 4: The Science of Playing and Recording

The helical scan method is a specialized technique used in VCRs to maximize the quantity of video data saved on a finite amount of magnetic tape. Helical scan records and reads data in diagonal stripes, rather than horizontal lines over the width of the tape, as one might assume. This method enables the VCR to store and retrieve a far higher density of information on the tape's surface, allowing it to record complete movies, shows, or records on a single cassette. This approach is critical to VHS technology because it maximizes the use of tape space, balancing storage capacity and quality to produce an economical, high-capacity video format.

The tilting drum is important to the helical scan procedure. The drum is set at a little inclination and rotates quickly, its magnetic heads reading the tape as it goes across. When the VHS tape is placed and wrapped around the

The drum produces a slanted path for the heads to follow, which exactly aligns with the diagonal recording stripes on the tape. The magnetic heads included in the revolving drum come into close contact with the tape, reading the data encoded along these diagonal lines to extract the video and audio signals required for playback.

The interaction of the drum and magnetic heads is a highly coordinated operation. As the tape goes slowly past the drum, the heads spin quickly, allowing them to make several passes across the tape's surface in a short period of time. Each head scans a thin, diagonal strip of magnetic data, capturing encoded information and transmitting it through the VCR's electronics to be decoded into images and sound. This quick spinning of the heads, together with the drum's slanted layout, guarantees that all video data is captured with great fidelity, despite the tape's relatively modest speed.

The drum and magnetic heads use helical scan technology to recover a continuous, flawless stream of visual and audio data from the tape. This synchronized movement is critical for providing a consistent, uninterrupted playback experience, allowing the VCR to display a seamless sequence of images and sounds on the screen. The helical scan method, with its economical use of space and precise reading capabilities, was a major innovation in VHS technology, allowing a single strip of magnetic tape to store complete films and play them back with clarity and consistency.

In a VCR, the audio and control track head is critical for controlling both sound and tracking information, ensuring that the video and audio remain synchronized throughout playback. Audio and control signals, unlike video data, are recorded on specified, linear areas of the tape, rather than diagonally across it. The audio data is stored at the top border of the cassette.

The control track runs along the bottom border. This separation allows the VCR to process both types of data independently but perfectly aligned, ensuring flawless synchronization between picture and sound.

The audio track records sound information, such as dialogue and music, and plays it back in rhythm with the visual material. The control track, on the other hand, serves as a guide for the VCR's playback speed, supplying critical timing information that allows the machine to maintain a consistent pace and position while reading the tape. This control track data is especially crucial when fast-forwarding, rewinding, or executing actions that require changes in tape speed because it allows the VCR to precisely track its position on the tape. The VCR may provide a smooth watching experience by using independent but coordinated audio and control tracks, ensuring that audio and video remain synced even when the tape is paused, sped up, or reversed.

The record tab mechanism on a VHS tape provides an additional layer of functionality and protection throughout the recording process. The record tab, located on the bottom edge of the VHS cassette, is a small, removable plastic piece that indicates whether a tape can be recorded. When the tab is intact, the VCR recognizes that the tape is recordable and allows users to record fresh content on it. However, if the tab is removed or damaged, the VCR's record sensor detects this and stops the recording function, preventing fresh information from being written to the tape.

This capability is notably handy for commercially manufactured tapes, such as movies and special recordings, which sometimes ship with the record tab already removed. By removing the tab, producers ensure that these tapes cannot be unintentionally recorded over, conserving the original content. This simple yet effective system offers users peace of mind by preventing cherished recordings or lucrative commercial tapes.

Avoid being wiped or overwritten. To re-enable recording on a tape with a removed tab, just cover the open tab slot with a little piece of tape, tricking the VCR into perceiving it as recordable again. This record tab mechanism provides a simple means to preserve content, making it an important aspect in the design of VHS cassettes.

Chapter 5: Fast Forward, Rewind, and Eject

The VCR's fast forward and rewind functions are based on a synchronized mechanism that engages various spools within the cassette to move the tape quickly in either direction. During normal playback, the capstan and pinch roller draw the tape steadily across the heads, allowing for smooth, controlled movement. When fast forward or rewind is selected, the VCR turns its attention to the spools on either side of the cassette—the supply reel and the take-up reel. In fast-forward mode, the VCR's motor engages the take-up reel, spinning it quickly to pull the tape from the supply reel and move it to the other side at a high pace. For rewind, the VCR reverses the operation, causing the supply reel to wind the tape back onto itself.

These high-speed actions bypass the capstan and pinch roller, instead relying on direct spool pull to wind the tape significantly faster. This structure enables users to move swiftly.

Go through the content or return to the beginning of the tape without having to wait for the regular playback speed. It also requires precise tension to keep the tape from loosening or tangling, which could damage the magnetic strip and reduce video quality.

VCRs have an LED light and end-of-tape sensors to keep the tape from snapping when it reaches the end during fast forwarding or rewinding. These sensors, located within the machine, work in conjunction with the LED light to determine when the magnetic tape has reached either end of the cassette. When a VHS tape is loaded, the magnetic tape blocks the light path between the LED and the sensors, indicating that the tape is still accessible to be played or wound. However, as the tape nears its endpoint, it displays a clear area with no magnetic coating. This clear part allows the LED light to travel through unhindered to the sensors on the other side.

When the sensors identify this clear section of tape, the VCR's control system instantly turns off the motor to prevent further movement. This function is critical for eliminating the possibility of snapping the tape, which may happen if the machine continues to pull on it after reaching the end. By responding to the clear tape section, the VCR guarantees that playback, fast forward, and rewind operations are completed smoothly, saving the tape from wear and tear over time. This sensor system, while simple, plays an important role in the longevity of both the tape and the VCR, allowing consumers to enjoy their content without fear of accidental harm.

When a user clicks the eject button on a VCR, the machine begins a thorough process of retracting the tape and preparing the VHS cassette for removal. This set of actions is essentially the opposite of the loading process, ensuring that the tape is properly returned to its cassette without causing damage or tangling.

First, the VCR disengages the capstan, pinch roller, and tension arms that keep the tape in place during playback. By releasing these components, the tape is no longer dragged or stretched over the different elements of the machine, allowing it to retract smoothly. The guide rollers, which had previously extracted the tape from the cassette and threaded it around the drum and reading heads, now reverse their direction. They gently guide the tape back into the cassette and wind it neatly onto the VHS supply reel.

As the tape retracts, the VCR carefully maintains the required tension to keep the tape from becoming loose or misaligned, which could cause problems the next time it is played. When the magnetic tape is entirely retracted into the cassette and the guide rollers have finished their return path, the spring-loaded door on the front of the

VHS cassette closes, shielding the tape from dust and damage.

After safely storing the tape within, the VCR lowers the cassette back into its original place in the loading tray. The tray extends outward, allowing the user to retrieve the tape safely. This well-coordinated ejection procedure guarantees that the tape is entirely retracted and the cassette is returned to its normal form, ready to be withdrawn from the VCR without causing harm.

Chapter 6: Unique features and enhancements

As VCR technology advanced, producers began to focus on improving audio quality, resulting in the introduction of Hi-Fi (high-fidelity) audio in later VCR models. Unlike traditional mono or linear stereo audio tracks, which were recorded along the tape's edge, Hi-Fi audio tracks were inserted within the video part of the tape itself, employing a pair of dedicated audio heads inside the revolving drum. This positioning enabled Hi-Fi audio to record a broader, richer sound with more fidelity, resulting in a substantially better listening experience. Hi-Fi enabled consumers to enjoy stereo sound equivalent to that heard on audio cassette cassettes or even compact discs, resulting in crisper conversation, more dynamic music, and a more immersive listening experience.

Hi-Fi audio enhanced the cinematic experience of watching movies at home by bringing professional-quality sound into the living room.

Hi-Fi VCRs could still play normal tapes, but the improved audio capabilities brought a new level of enjoyment to those who had Hi-Fi-compatible records. This function made Hi-Fi VCRs especially popular among moviegoers and families that valued high-quality sound, as the richer audio enhanced the visual experience and brought movies to life in ways that previous VCR models could not.

Along with audio enhancements, advanced VCR models added technologies such as auto-tracking and picture stabilization to increase playback quality. Tracking refers to the alignment of the VCR's heads with the video data captured on tape. In early VCR devices, users had to manually adjust the tracking to reduce visual distortions like lines or flickering, especially if the tape was old or recorded on a different machine. However, auto-tracking technology enabled the VCR to detect and modify the alignment automatically, removing the need for manual corrections.

Assuring a sharper, more steady image. This feature improved playback by removing one of the most prevalent hassles associated with watching videos on a VCR.

Picture stabilization was another enhancement designed to reduce visual disruptions. This feature assisted in repairing minor flaws or shakiness in the video stream, resulting in a smoother and more consistent viewing experience. Picture stabilization improved the VCR's capacity to produce a consistent image by automatically compensating for minor differences in the movement of the tape, even on tapes that had worn over time. These advancements in Hi-Fi audio, auto-tracking, and picture stabilization transformed the VCR from a simple playback device to a refined, high-quality entertainment system, making home video viewing more enjoyable and accessible to a larger audience.

One of the most popular features in advanced VCR

models was the ability to arrange timers.

Recordings, a feature that lets customers record specific shows without being physically there. With timer recording, users could program the VCR to start recording a show at a specific time and channel. This feature was especially useful for those who didn't want to miss their favorite show or a live event that aired at an inconvenient time. Users could record shows even if they weren't at home by setting the timer, and the VCR would start and stop recording based on the settings they provided. This feature was a game changer, giving consumers greater control and flexibility over their TV viewing schedules and offering a more personalized viewing experience.

In addition to timed recording, several VCRs included playback and recording modes such as Standard Play (SP) and Long Play (LP). These modes let users select video quality and recording length based on their preferences. SP mode offered the maximum possible video quality.

It produced crisper visuals and better sound, but it also required more tape, limiting the recording length to around two hours per normal VHS cassette. LP mode, on the other hand, significantly reduced the quality while increasing the recording time to roughly four hours, making it perfect for longer recordings such as movies or sporting events. Some VCRs also had an Extended Play (EP) mode, which allowed for up to six hours of recording on a single tape, but the video quality was substantially inferior.

Aside from these core features, some VCRs incorporated other useful features such as parental controls to prohibit particular channels or programs, on-screen menus to make navigation easier, and even channel memory presets that allowed the VCR to recall regularly recorded channels. These added features helped to make the VCR more adaptable and user-friendly, allowing it to meet a wide range of requirements and preferences. By providing capabilities such as timed recording, customizable playback settings, and intuitive

VCRs evolved into powerful home entertainment gadgets, allowing consumers to personalize their viewing experiences in groundbreaking ways at the time.

Chapter 7: The Legacy of the VCR

VCRs revolutionized entertainment consumption by giving consumers unprecedented control over what and when they viewed it. Before VCRs, individuals were constrained to TV network schedules and could only watch movies in theaters. The VCR changed all of that, allowing viewers to record television shows, relive their favorite moments, and, most significantly, watch movies and series whenever they wanted. This newfound flexibility altered the interaction between audiences and media, allowing people to plan entertainment around their own schedules. The ability to record programs for later watching eliminated the need for people to alter their calendars to catch a specific show, resulting in what we now refer to as time-shifted viewing—a forerunner to today's on-demand streaming culture.

VCRs did more than only shift viewing patterns; they also transformed homes into personal movie theaters. With

Video rental stores Increasing in popularity throughout the 1980s and 1990s, families could bring home their favorite films and watch them frequently, resulting in movie evenings in the comfort of their living rooms. This was a cultural revolution, as consumers were no longer reliant on the theatrical experience for new releases. Instead, consumers could create personal libraries of rented or purchased VHS cassettes, rewatching old favorites and discovering new ones at their leisure. This invention democratized media access, allowing more individuals to interact with a wide range of content that was previously unavailable.

In addition to their influence on viewing habits, VCRs became cultural icons, representing the do-it-yourself approach to home entertainment. The classic "Be Kind, Rewind" stickers on rental tapes acted as a reminder of the communal component of VHS usage, with courteous renters ensuring that the video was rewound and ready to go for the next person. This modest deed became an emblem of the VHS era.

Etiquette is a tribute to the common experience of renting and returning recordings. VCRs also became part of the background of innumerable family memories, from recorded holiday gatherings to hours of childhood cartoons saved on tape, providing a personal dimension to their cultural significance.

Today, VCRs have a nostalgic appeal for individuals who grew up in the 1980s and 1990s. The tactile experience of loading a tape, the machine's familiar hum, and the somewhat grainy quality of VHS playback all elicit feelings of comfort and nostalgia for simpler times. For many, the VCR symbolizes a watershed moment in entertainment history, when people first gained control over what they watched and began to assemble personal libraries of their favorite movies and shows. Though VCRs have long since been supplanted by DVDs, Blu-rays, and digital streaming, they remain an iconic emblem of a time when the home entertainment revolution began, leaving behind.

An enduring legacy that continues to evoke good recollections and pique the interest of new generations.

Even in today's digital age, VCRs and VHS tapes remain popular among enthusiasts and collectors who value the tactile connection and memories they bring. For many, VCRs reflect the early days of home entertainment—a time when owning a favorite movie or recording a beloved TV show felt like a personal accomplishment. Unlike today's streaming systems, when access is transitory and titles disappear without notice, VHS tapes provide a persistent, hands-on experience. Holding a VHS tape, inserting it into a VCR, and watching the familiar replay provides a sense of continuity and connection that is grounded and genuine. The grainy pictures and old sound have a charming quality that transports viewers back to simpler times when watching a movie seemed intentional and memorable.

Collectors view VHS cassettes as more than simply movies or shows; they are artifacts of cultural history. VHS tape covers, which are frequently covered with unique artwork, have their own aesthetic significance, especially in an era when tangible media is becoming increasingly scarce. Collectors like the thrill of discovering rare titles, distinctive covers, or old family recordings that have not been digitized, making each cassette a potential treasure. Furthermore, VHS cassettes may contain content that is not available on modern streaming services, such as vintage movies, shows, or local TV broadcasts. This makes VCRs and VHS collections extremely significant for those who value media that isn't readily available elsewhere, preserving pieces of history that may otherwise be lost.

Despite their enduring appeal, VHS cassettes will inevitably degrade over time. Temperature and humidity can cause wear, fading, and damage to the magnetic tape within a cassette.

And frequent use. For individuals who value their home recordings, such as family gatherings, childhood milestones, and personal memories, digital storage provides a way to protect these important moments. Converting VHS tapes to digital format assures that these memories are retained in a long-lasting format, free of magnetic tape's physical restrictions. This process can be carried out by professional transfer services or at home with very inexpensive equipment, converting aged VHS footage into digital data that can be readily stored, shared, and backed up across devices.

Embracing digital storage allows consumers to have the best of both worlds—retaining the nostalgic and aesthetic value of their VHS collections while keeping crucial recordings in a secure, long-term format. In this way, enthusiasts can honor the legacy of VCRs and VHS tapes while ensuring that unique memories are preserved, retaining the spirit of the analog period for future generations to appreciate and enjoy.

Conclusion

The VCR marks an intriguing phase in the history of home entertainment, a time when analog technology instilled a distinct feeling of enchantment and wonder in homes. Unlike today's digital devices, VCRs were complex machines with many moving parts, each designed to operate together to convert magnetic signals into moving images and sound. There was a palpable link to the viewing experience, from inserting the tape to hearing the machine's hum and seeing the visuals come to life on screen. The VCR epitomized the ethos of an era that valued hands-on technology and relished the excitement of recording, rewinding, and rewatching favorite moments. Its appeal lay in its simplicity and brilliance, portraying an experience that, while no longer popular, nonetheless evokes nostalgia and intrigue.

The VCR left an indisputable legacy. It was a tipping moment in how people consumed media.

Giving audiences control over what and when they watch. It made entertainment more personal and accessible, paving the way for new forms like DVDs and, eventually, digital streaming. By allowing consumers to develop personal collections, preserve family memories, and even discover rare or specialized content, the VCR transformed home viewing, laying the groundwork for today's media ecosystem. Although it may appear archaic in comparison to today's high-definition, on-demand possibilities, the VCR has had a long-lasting and deep impact on the entertainment business and everyday life.

Looking ahead, the value of conserving analog media is becoming increasingly evident. As physical formats disappear in favor of digital convenience, attempts to save older media such as VHS tapes are critical to preserving our cultural legacy. Digitizing VHS tapes and other formats allows us to preserve memories, family recordings, and historical videos that would otherwise be lost.

On time. By preserving these analog treasures, we may share the charm, relevance, and experiences of previous generations with future generations. The VCR may have outlived its usefulness, but its legacy continues to inspire, reminding us that the value of technology lies not just in its functionality, but also in the memories and connections it fosters.